COMMUNITY HELPERS

DOCTORS

Written by Eliza Nodes

I0867512

Genius Kid

This edition is published by arrangement with BookLife Publishing

sales@northstareditions.com | 888-417-0195

Library of Congress Control Number:
2025943067

ISBN
979-8-89471-050-1 (library bound)
979-8-89471-070-9 (paperback)
979-8-89471-109-6 (epub)
979-8-89471-090-7 (hosted ebook)

Printed in the United States of America
Mankato, MN
012026

Written by:
Eliza Nodes

Edited by:
Rebecca Phillips-Bartlett

Designed by:
Ker Ker Lee

Photo Credits – Images courtesy of Shutterstock.com, unless otherwise stated.

Cover – New Africa, 9dream studio, Tarzhanova, Strakhov Pavel, SebGross, Barvista, ImageFlow. 2–3 – New Africa, Prostock-studio, Pressmaster. 4–5 – Just dance, pakww. 6–7 – Ljupco Smokovski, Brian A Jackson. 8–9 – StockImageFactory.com, KOTOIMAGES, AnnaStills. 10–11 – fonok, frank333, Blaj Gabriel, all_about_people. 12–13 – Ground Picture, masa44, Fotos593. 14–15 – oscarloperamartos, LightField Studios. 16–17 – mizy, faestock, Korrapon Karapan, spatuletail, Dmitrijs Kaminskis, Iryna Pohrebna. 18–19 – Prostock-studio, Master of Stocks. 20–21 – Satirus, frank60, Pressmaster,Peter Hermes Furian. 22–23 – paulista, chomplearn, Komsan Loonprom, Ljupco Smokovski, Odua Images.

CONTENTS

Page 4	Doctors
Page 6	Many Jobs in One
Page 10	At the Hospital
Page 12	Equipment
Page 16	A History of Doctors
Page 18	Becoming a Doctor
Page 20	Believe It or Not!
Page 22	Are You a Genius Kid?
Page 24	Glossary and Index

Words that look like this can be found in the glossary on page 24.

DOCTORS

When you think of a doctor, what do you see?

Do you see someone wearing a uniform? Is that person holding a clipboard or tablet?

Doctors are important members of the community. They help people who are ill or hurt.

DID YOU KNOW?
Most doctors wear uniforms called scrubs. Many also wear white coats.

Some doctors take an oath. An oath is a serious promise. Doctors promise to not harm anyone.

DID YOU KNOW?
The oath some doctors take is called the Hippocratic Oath.

MANY JOBS IN ONE

Doctors do many different jobs.

EXAMINING PATIENTS

Patients are people who receive medical care. Doctors ask them questions. They check patients' symptoms. Symptoms are signs of an illness or injury. Doctors try to find out what's wrong.

WRITING RECORDS

Doctors keep records. Records include lists of patients' symptoms. They also include diagnoses and treatment plans. Other doctors and nurses use the records. They help treat the same patients.

DID YOU KNOW?

A diagnosis is when an illness or injury is identified.

TREATMENT PLANS

Doctors create plans for treatment. Treatment plans might include giving out medicine. Others include telling patients to do exercises. Some treatment plans include surgery.

INTERNS

Interns are new doctors. They finished medical school. Next, they start working in a hospital. They continue their education by helping treat patients.

TEACHING PEOPLE

Some doctors teach people how to look after themselves. This can help people avoid some illnesses and injuries.

AT THE HOSPITAL

Hospitals are made up of different parts called departments.

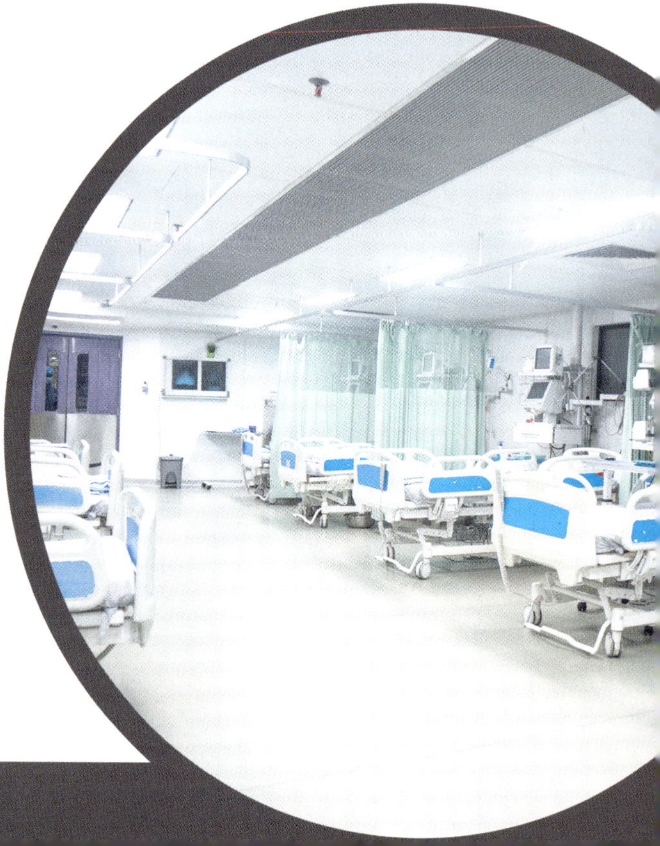

INTENSIVE CARE UNIT

People who are very seriously hurt stay in the intensive care unit. They need to be constantly watched by nurses and doctors.

EMERGENCY DEPARTMENT

People who have sudden injuries or illnesses go to the emergency department.

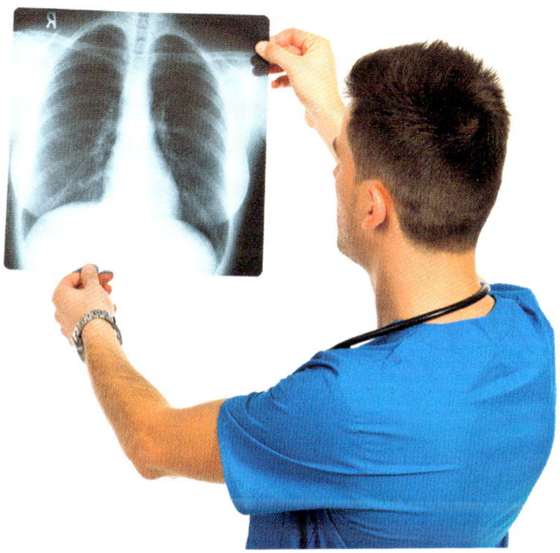

RADIOLOGY DEPARTMENT

Sometimes doctors need to see inside a patient's body. Doctors in radiology can use machines to scan a patient's bones and organs.

PEDIATRIC DEPARTMENT

Doctors in the pediatric department look after babies, children, and teenagers.

EQUIPMENT

Doctors use different types of equipment to do their job.

Face masks help doctors stay healthy while treating sick patients.

DID YOU KNOW?

Germs are tiny living things that can cause illnesses.

Gloves stop germs from spreading between doctors and patients. Doctors must wear gloves when they touch a patient.

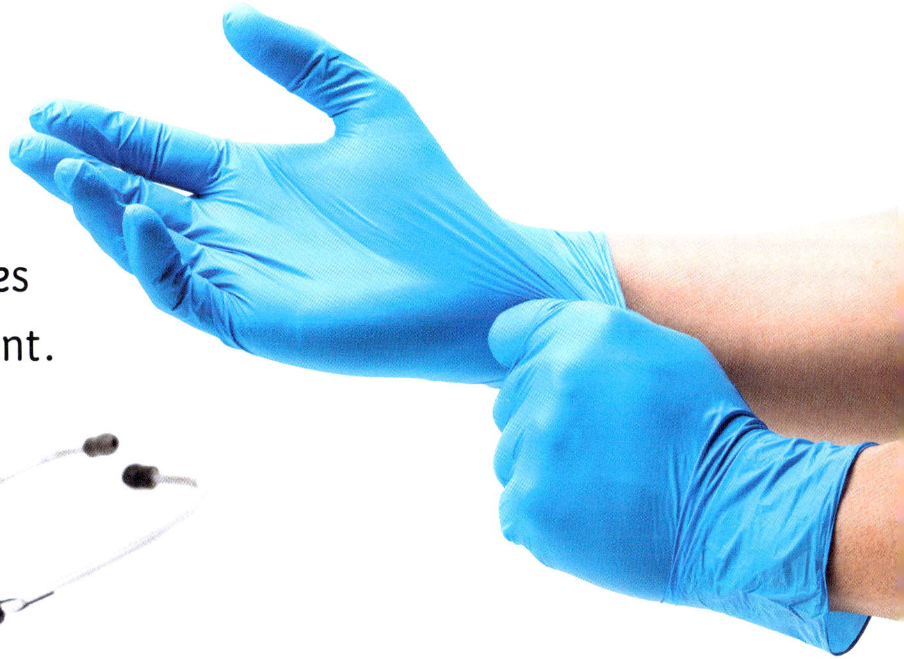

Doctors use stethoscopes. They listen to sounds inside the body. They may listen to a patient's heart or lungs.

Doctors use penlights. These small lights can check if a patient's eyes are working correctly. Doctors also use penlights to see things more clearly. For example, they can shine the penlight at the back of a patient's throat.

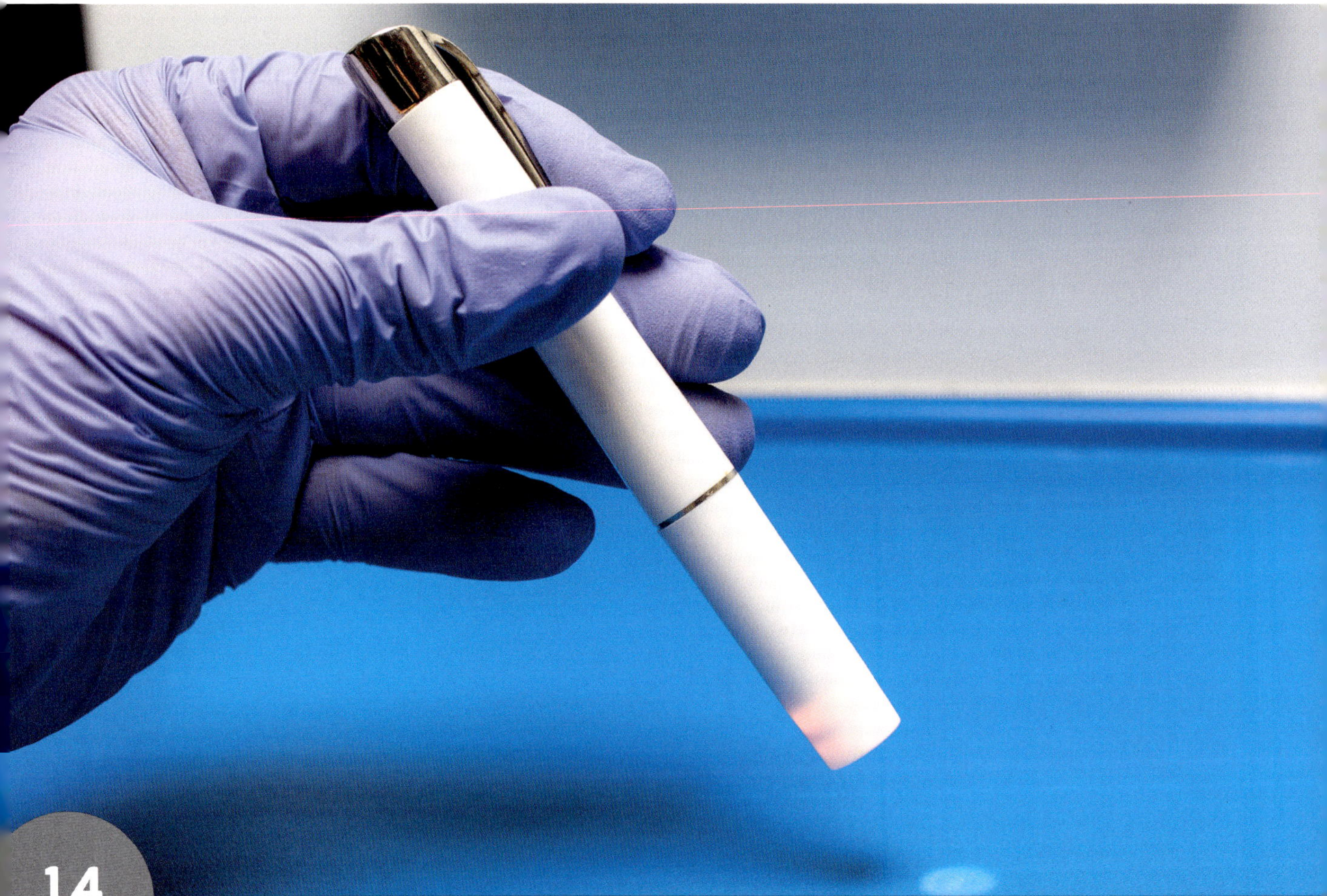

Doctors sometimes use reflex hammers on patients. A doctor can tap a patient's knee with the hammer. The patient's leg should kick. This means the patient's reflexes are working.

DID YOU KNOW?

Reflexes are ways the body automatically responds to certain things.

A HISTORY OF DOCTORS

Around 500–300 BCE

The Hippocratic Oath was written by a man called Hippocrates.

1766

The Medical Society of New Jersey formed. It taught people about health and medicine. It is the oldest medical organization in the United States.

1100–1300 CE

Some of the first medical schools were opened across Europe.

1849
Elizabeth Blackwell became the first woman in the United States to become a doctor.

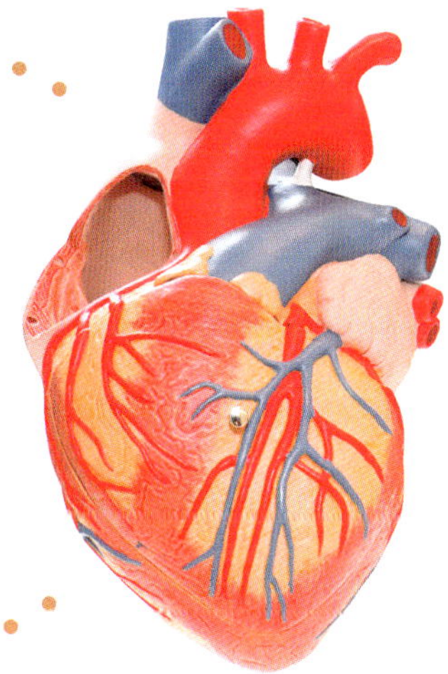

1967
The first human heart transplant was performed successfully.

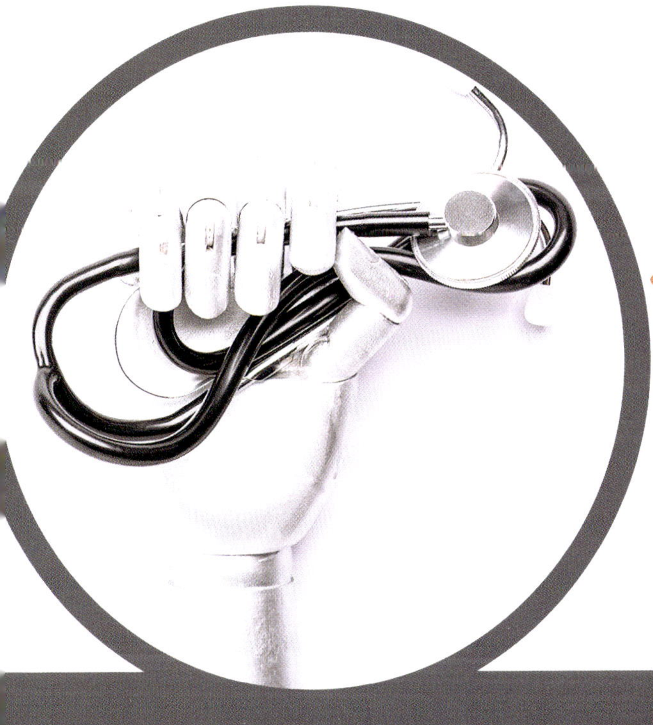

1985
A robot was used to perform surgery on a person for the first time.

BECOMING A DOCTOR

It takes many years to become a doctor. First, people must study science at college. Then, they go to medical school. When they finish, they become doctors. They start practicing as interns.

Doctors spend a lot of time talking to people. Doctors must learn how to <u>communicate</u> well.

Some people might be in pain. Doctors need to stay calm. They must work well under pressure. This can help people feel calm, too.

BELIEVE IT OR NOT!

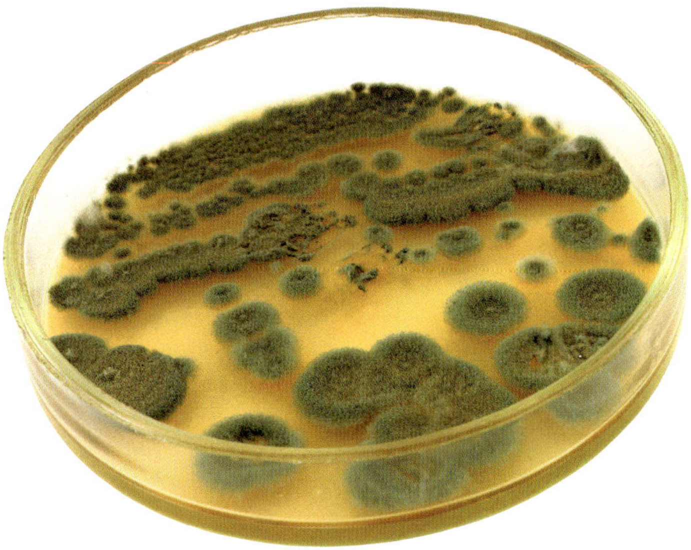

Some medicines have been discovered by accident. Dr. Alexander Fleming discovered penicillin when he forgot to clean up an experiment. Penicillin has saved millions of lives.

For many years, doctors removed patients' blood to try to cure illnesses. Sometimes the blood was sucked out by leeches.

Leech

Virtual reality goggles allow people to imagine they are somewhere else. Some medical students use these goggles. They can see images of the inside of the human body.

ARE YOU A GENIUS KID?

Now you have lots of fantastic doctor facts to amaze your friends and family. But first, let's see what you can remember. It is time to see whether you really are a genius kid.

Check back through the book if you are not sure.

1. What is the name of the oath many doctors take?
2. How do doctors examine patients?
3. When was the first successful human heart transplant performed?

Answers:
1. Hippocratic Oath, 2. Ask the patients questions and check for symptoms, 3. 1967.

GLOSSARY

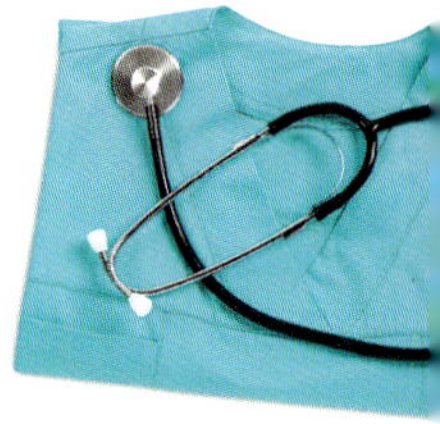

BCE	Before Common Era, the time before the year 0
communicate	to pass information between two or more people
community	a group of people who are connected by something
cure	to heal and make someone healthy again
equipment	items that are needed to complete a certain job
organization	a group of people who work together toward a specific goal or for a specific purpose
organs	parts of a living thing, such as the heart or lungs, that perform specific, important jobs
surgery	medical operations to repair, replace, or remove ill or injured parts o the body
transplant	when an organ is taken from one person's body and put into someone else's body

INDEX

hearts 13, 17
hospitals 9–11
illnesses 6–7, 9, 11–12, 21
injuries 6–7, 9, 11
leeches 21
oaths 5, 16
penicillin 20
records 7
students 21
symptoms 6–7